ALL I WANT FOR CHRISTMAS IS MY TWO FRONT TEETH

Words and Music by
DON GARDNER

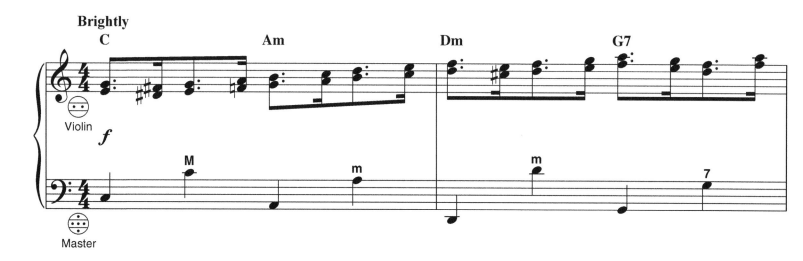

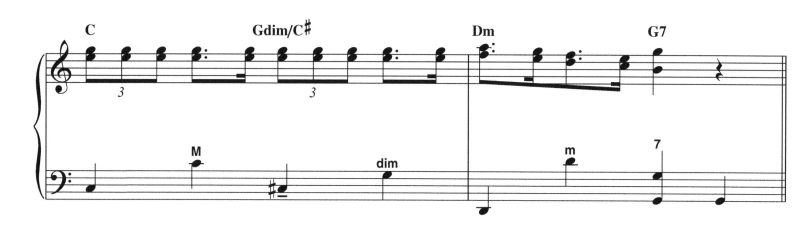

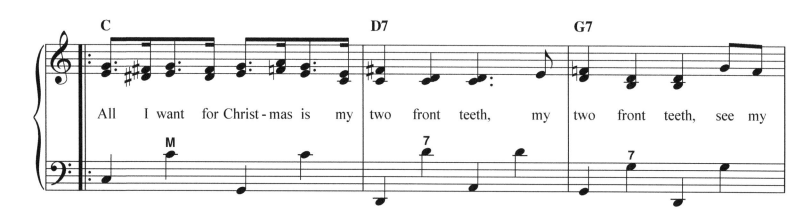

All I want for Christ-mas is my two front teeth, my two front teeth, see my

THE
Christmas Accordion
SONGBOOK

ISBN 978-1-4950-2587-7

HAL•LEONARD®
CORPORATION
7777 W. BLUEMOUND RD. P.O. BOX 13819 MILWAUKEE, WI 53213

Visit Hal Leonard Online at
www.halleonard.com

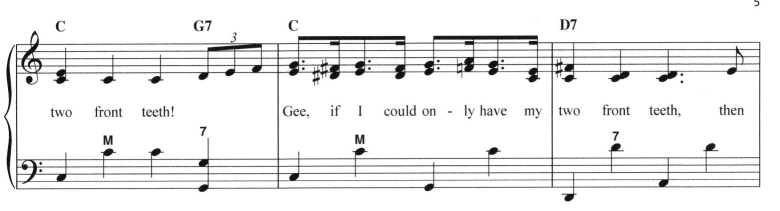

two front teeth! Gee, if I could on - ly have my two front teeth, then

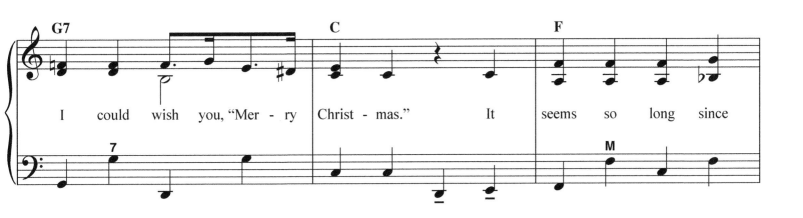

I could wish you, "Mer - ry Christ - mas." It seems so long since

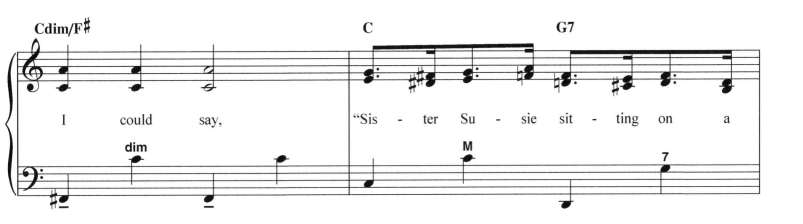

I could say, "Sis - ter Su - sie sit - ting on a

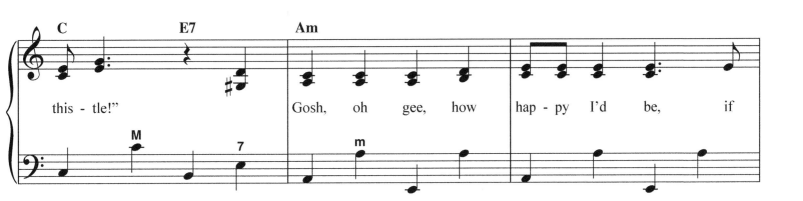

this - tle!" Gosh, oh gee, how hap - py I'd be, if

6

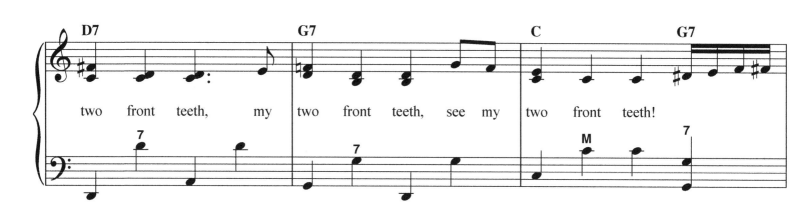

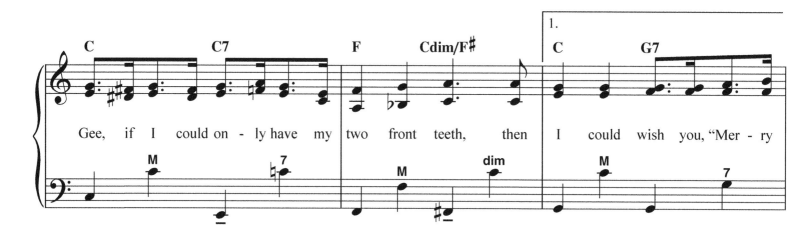

CAROLING, CAROLING

Words by WIHLA HUTSON
Music by ALFRED BURT

With a lilt

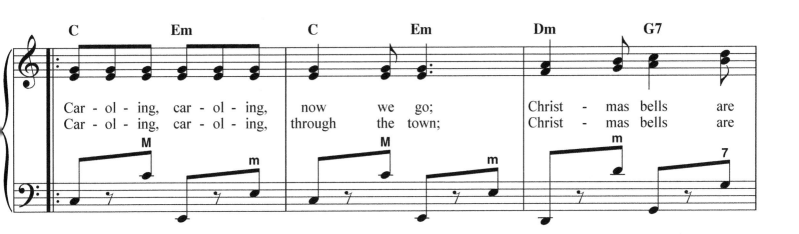

Car - ol - ing, car - ol - ing, now we go;
Car - ol - ing, car - ol - ing, through the town;
Christ - mas bells are
Christ - mas bells are

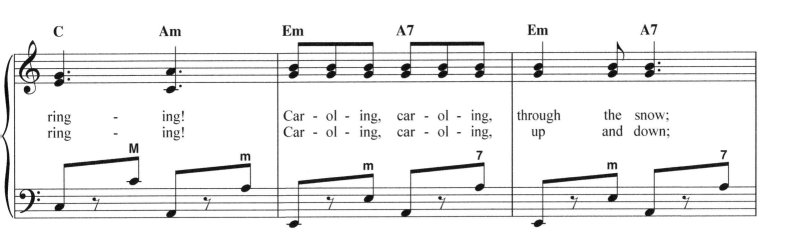

ring - ing!
ring - ing!
Car - ol - ing, car - ol - ing, through the snow;
Car - ol - ing, car - ol - ing, up and down;

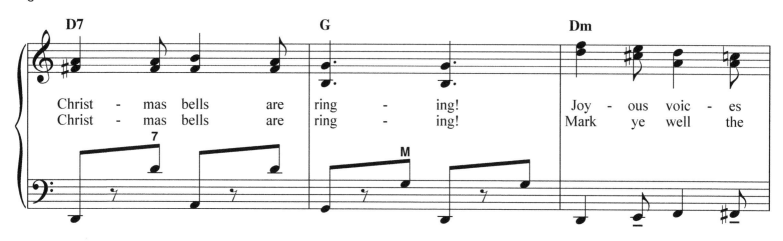

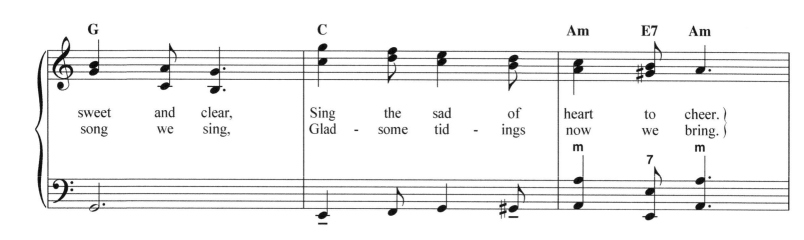

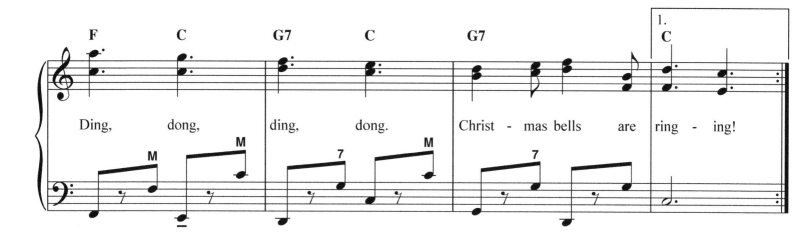

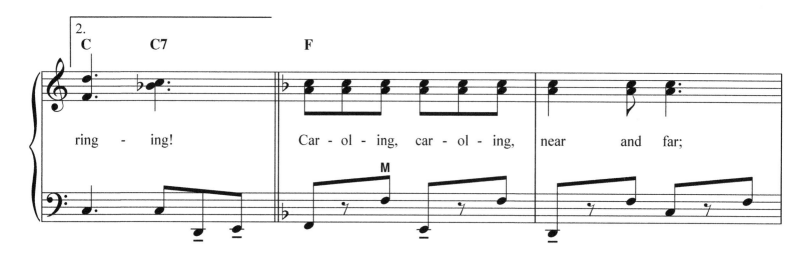

DO YOU HEAR WHAT I HEAR

Words and Music by NOEL REGNEY
and GLORIA SHAYNE

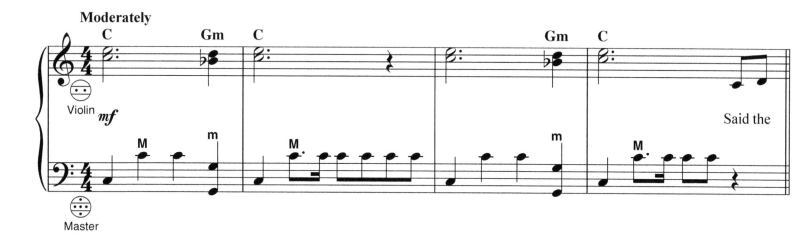

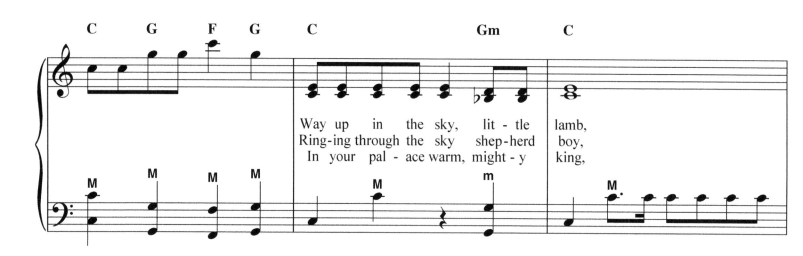

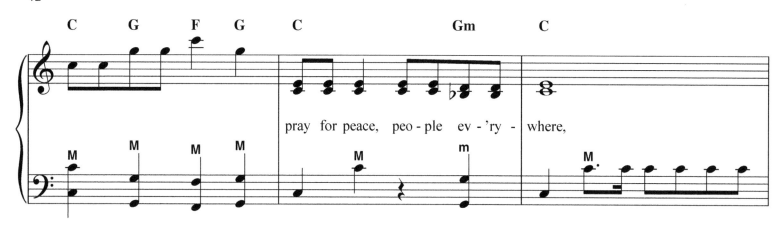

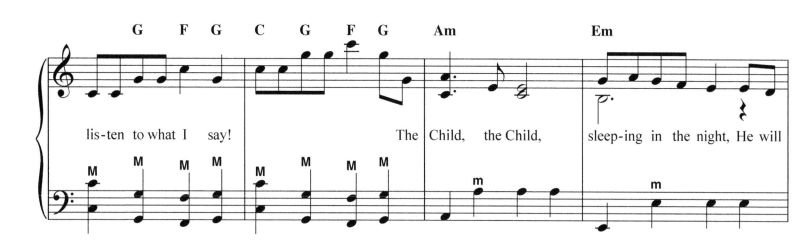

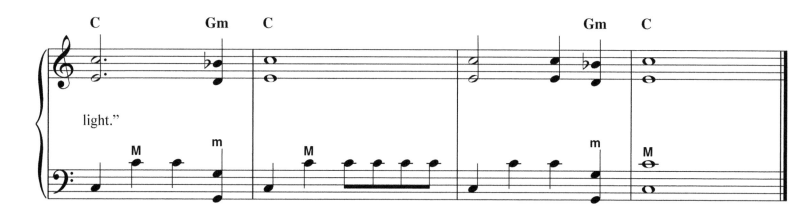

HAPPY XMAS
(War Is Over)

Written by JOHN LENNON
and YOKO ONO

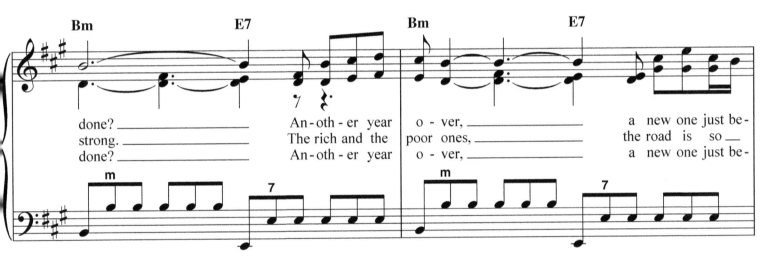

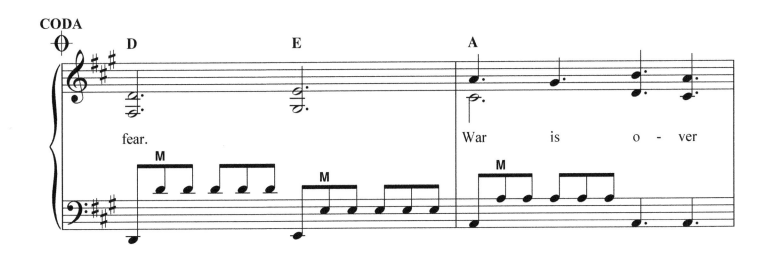

HAVE YOURSELF A MERRY LITTLE CHRISTMAS

from MEET ME IN ST. LOUIS

Words and Music by HUGH MARTIN
and RALPH BLANE

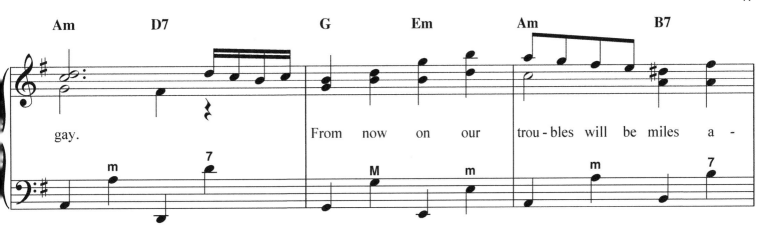

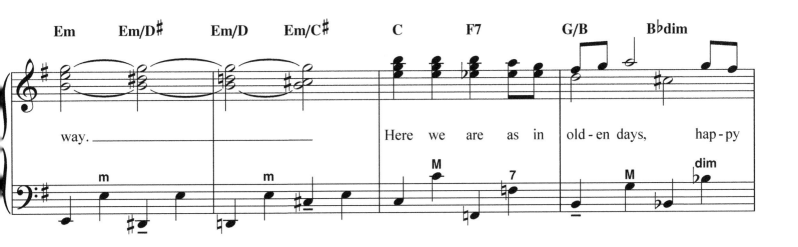

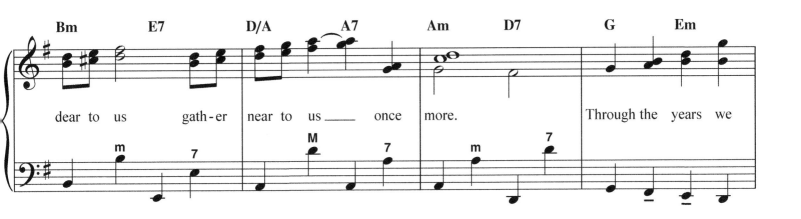

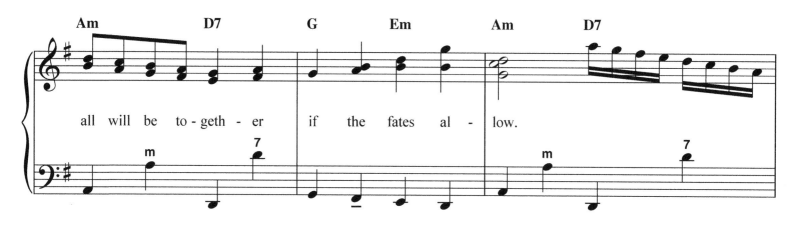

all will be to - geth - er   if   the   fates   al - low.

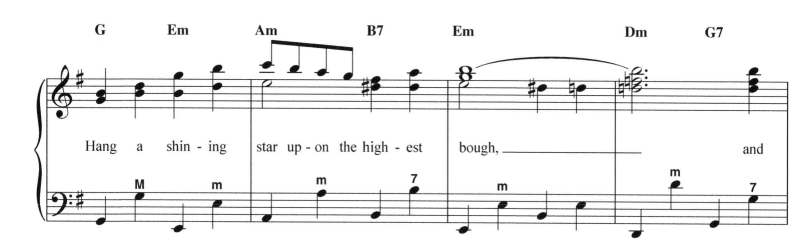

Hang   a   shin - ing   star up - on the high - est   bough, _____   and

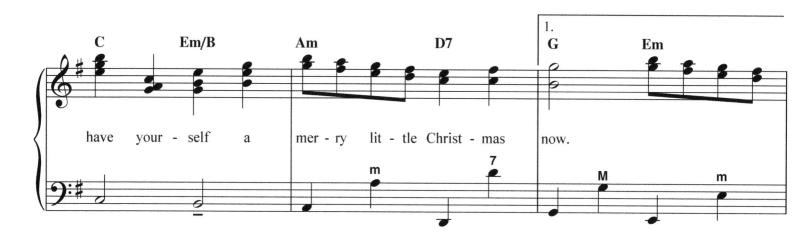

have   your - self   a   mer - ry   lit - tle   Christ - mas   now.

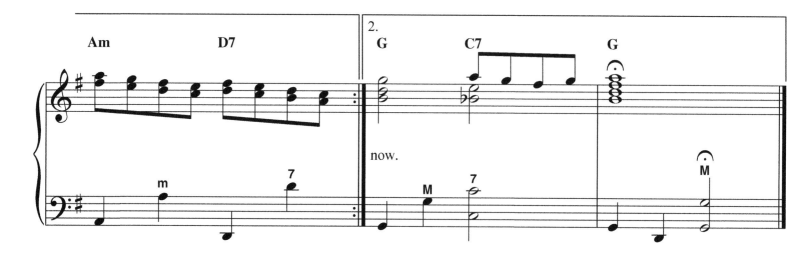

now.

THE LITTLE DRUMMER BOY

Words and Music by HARRY SIMEONE,
HENRY ONORATI and KATHERINE DAVIS

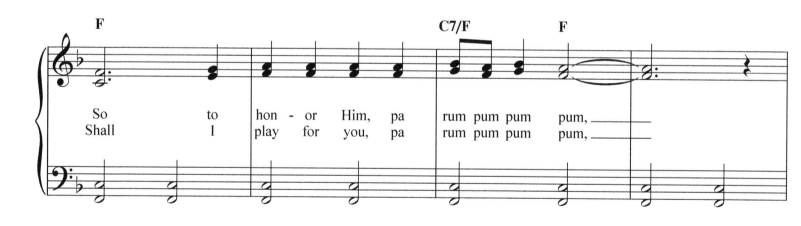

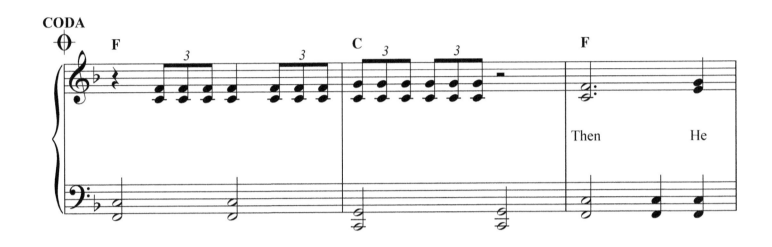

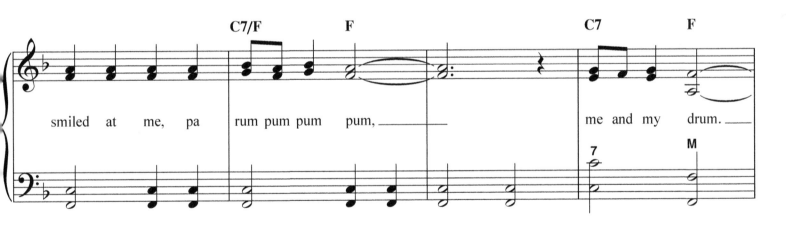

I WONDER AS I WANDER

By JOHN JACOB NILES

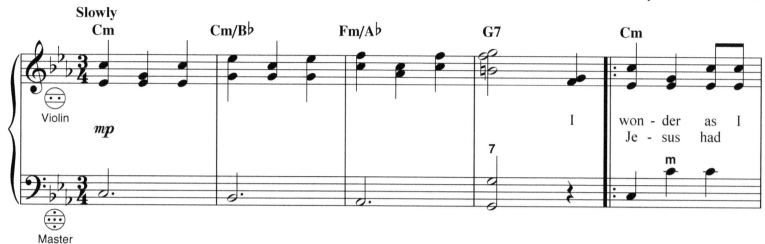

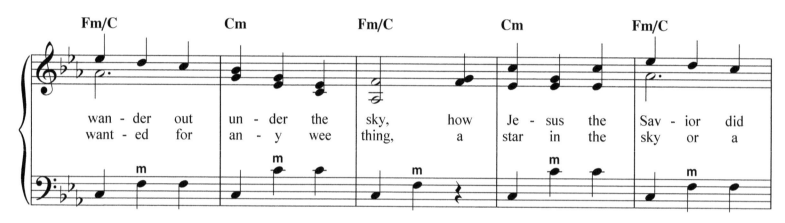

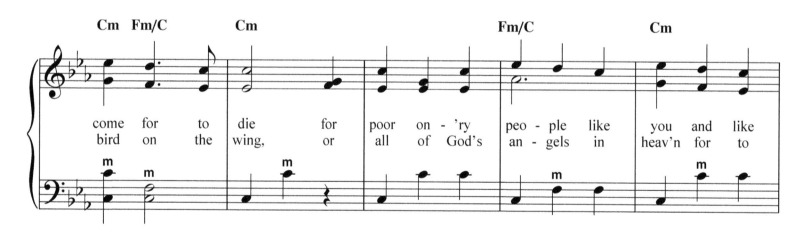

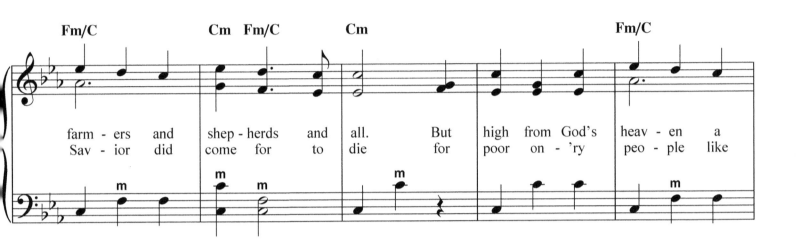

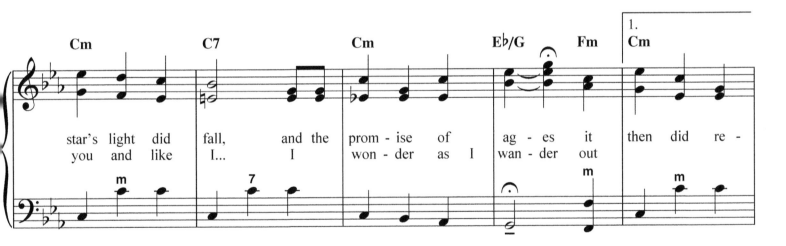

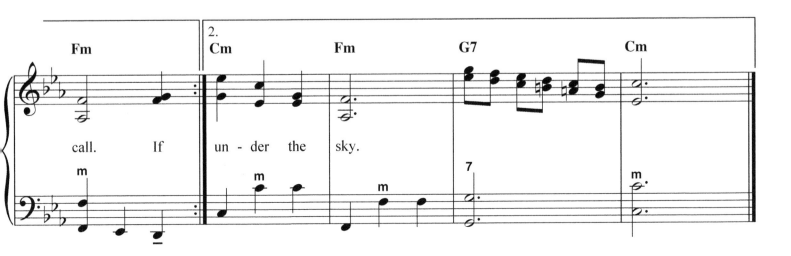

LAST CHRISTMAS

Words and Music by
GEORGE MICHAEL

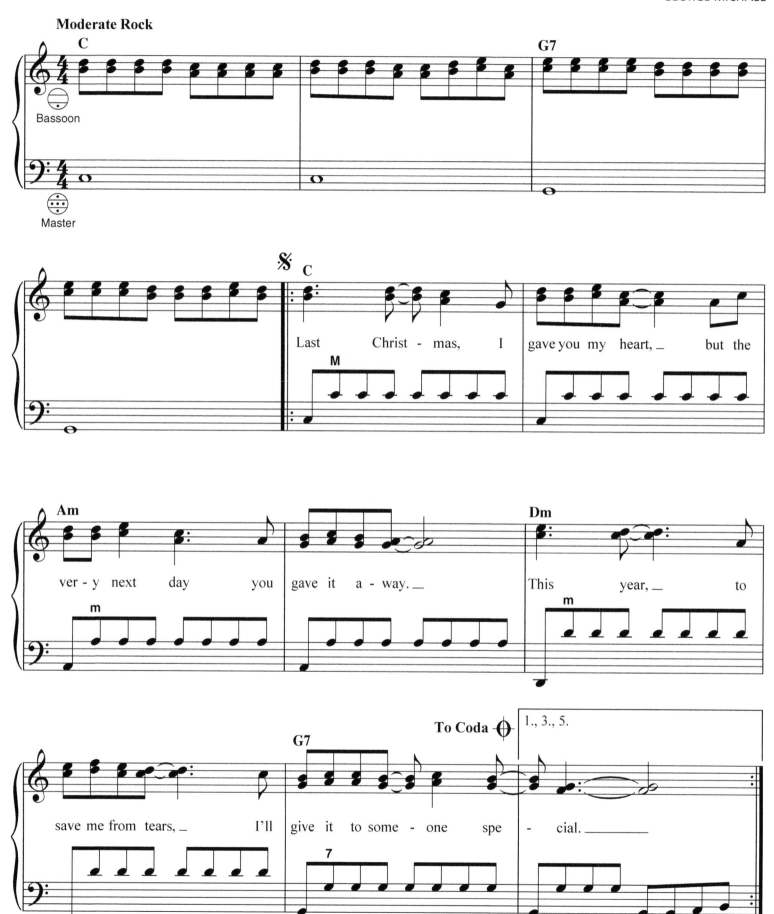

Last Christ - mas, I gave you my heart, _ but the ver - y next day you gave it a - way. _ This year, _ to save me from tears, _ I'll give it to some - one spe - cial. _____

Tell me, ba - by, do you rec - og - nize me?
My God, I thought you were some - one to re - ly on.

Well, it's been a year. It
Me, I guess I was a

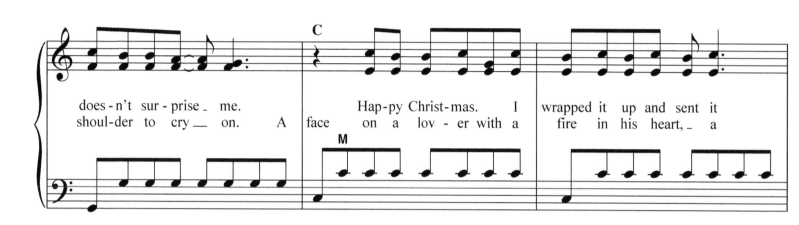

does - n't sur - prise _ me.
shoul - der to cry _ on. A

Hap - py Christ - mas. I
face on a lov - er with a

wrapped it up and sent it
fire in his heart, _ a

with a note say - ing, "I _ love you." I meant it.
man un - der cov - er but you tore me a - part. _

now _ I know _ what a fool _
I've been. But if you
Oo, _ now I've

kissed me now _ I know you'd
found a real love. You'll nev - er

fool me a - gain. _

LITTLE SAINT NICK

Words and Music by BRIAN WILSON
and MIKE LOVE

Mer - ry Christ-mas, Saint Nick.

Ooh.

Well, way up north where the
lit - tle bob - sled we call it
haul - in' through the snow at a

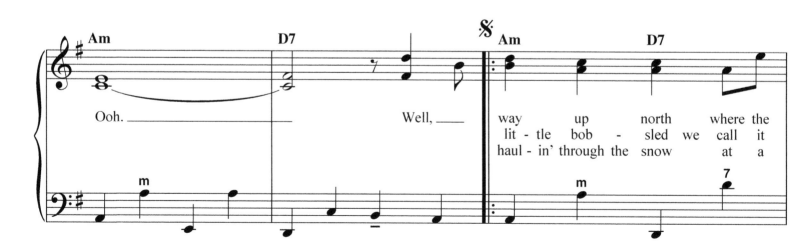

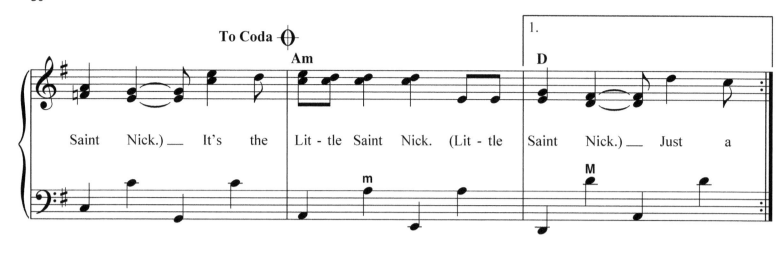

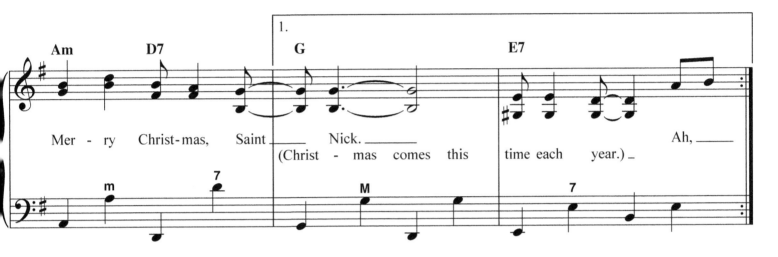

MARY, DID YOU KNOW?

Words and Music by MARK LOWRY
and BUDDY GREENE

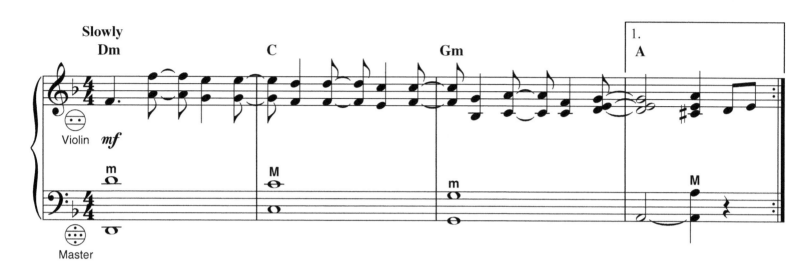

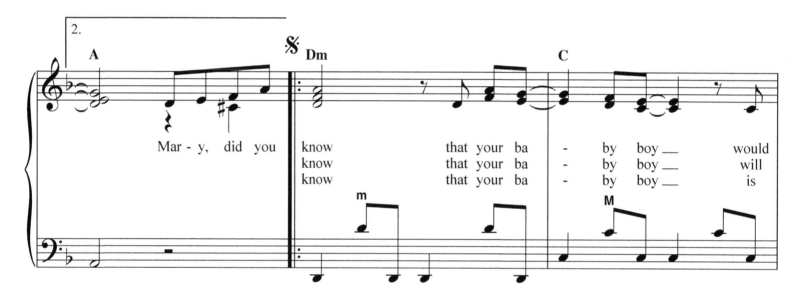

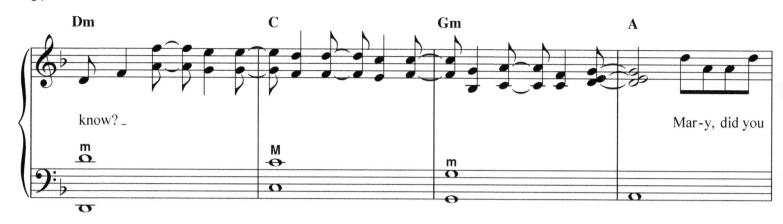

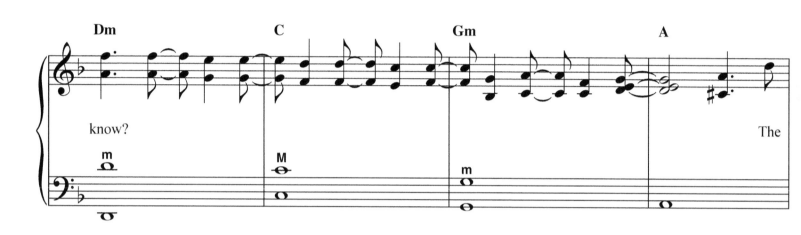

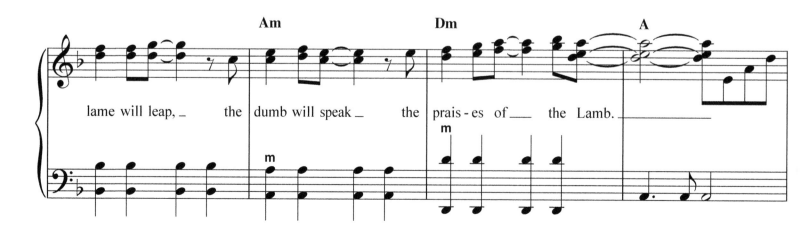

THE MOST WONDERFUL TIME OF THE YEAR

Words and Music by EDDIE POLA
and GEORGE WYLE

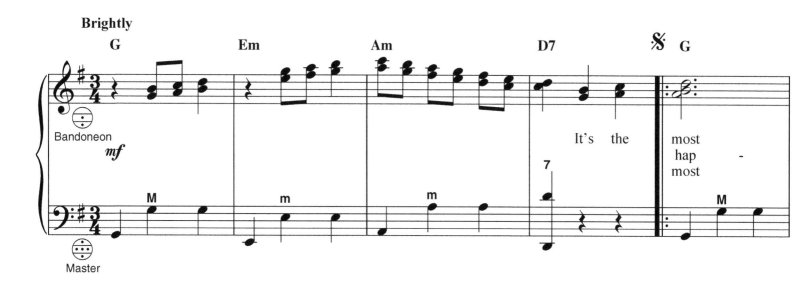

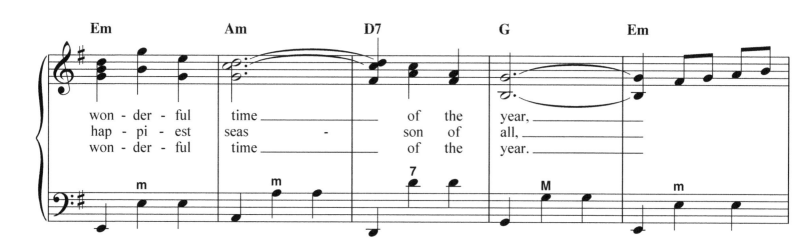

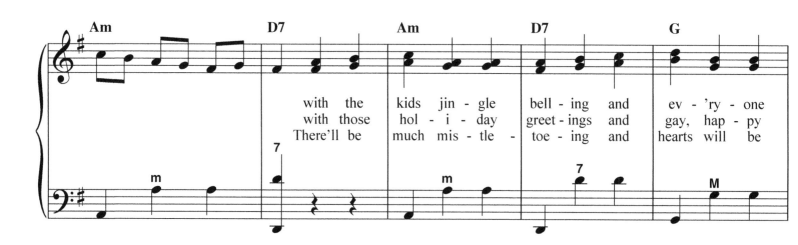

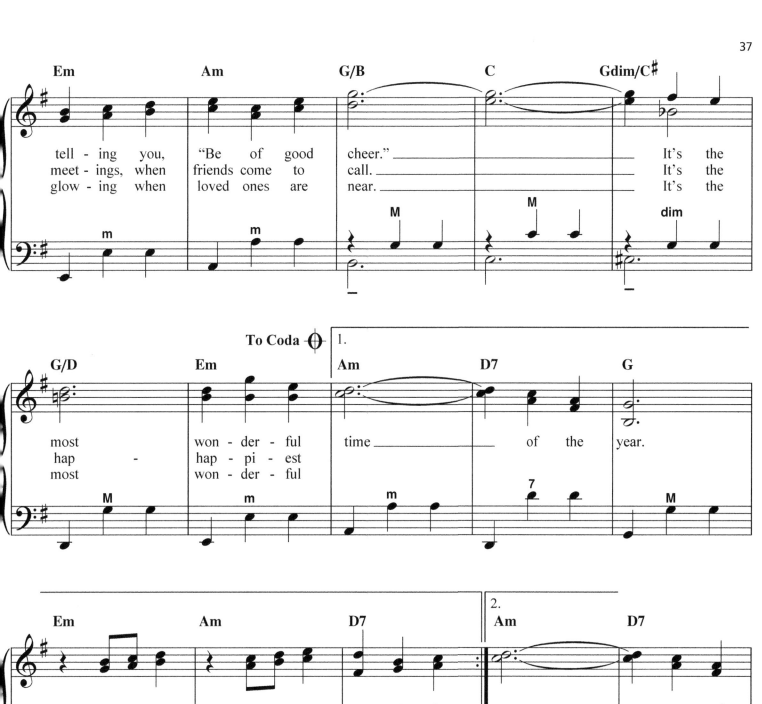

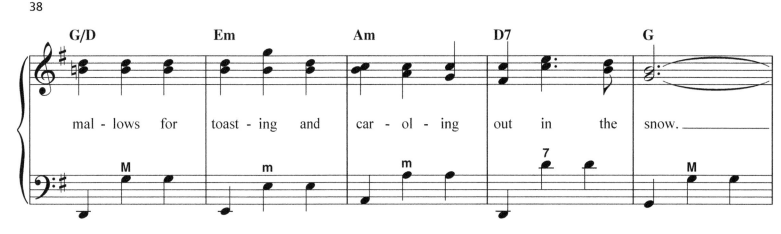

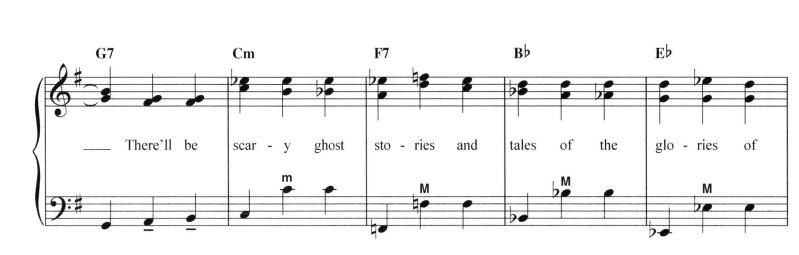

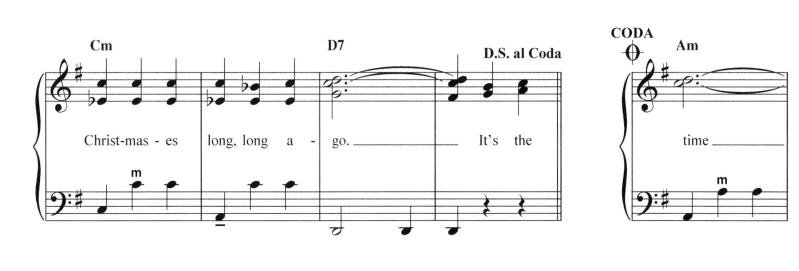

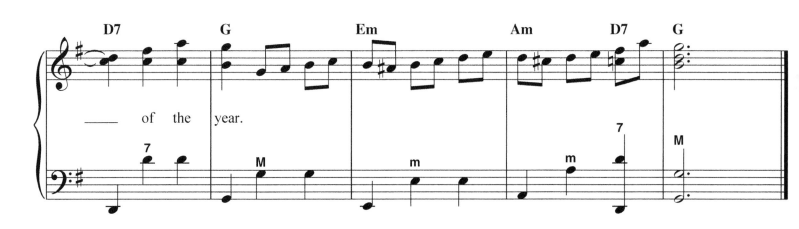

SILVER BELLS
from the Paramount Picture THE LEMON DROP KID

Words and Music by JAY LIVINGSTON
and RAY EVANS

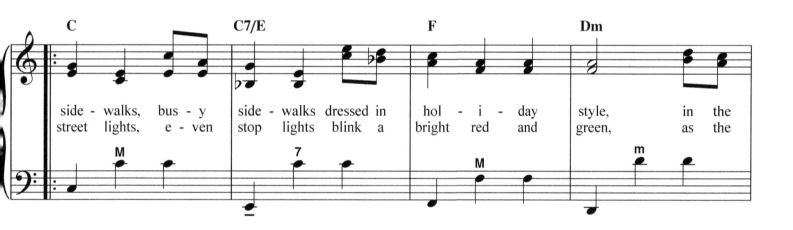

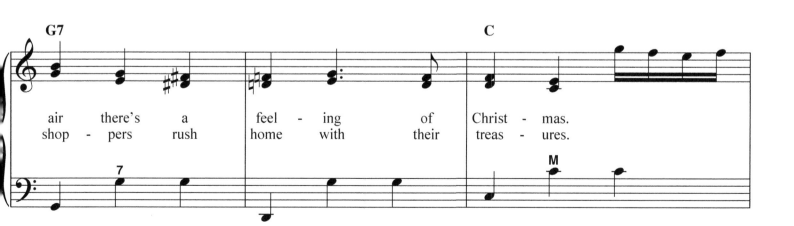

40

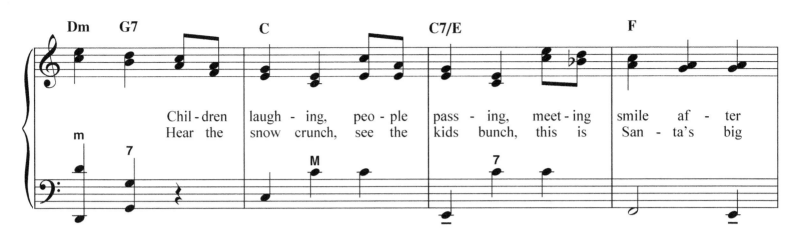

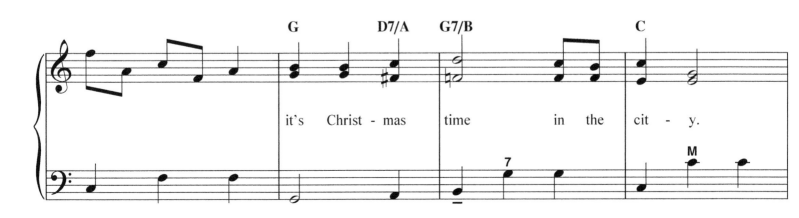

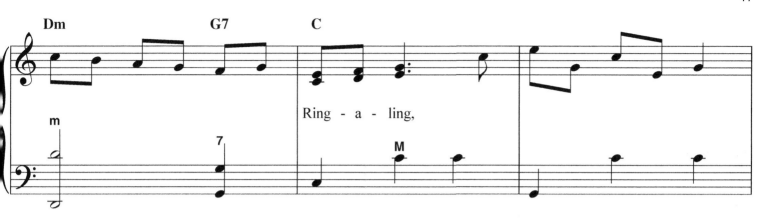

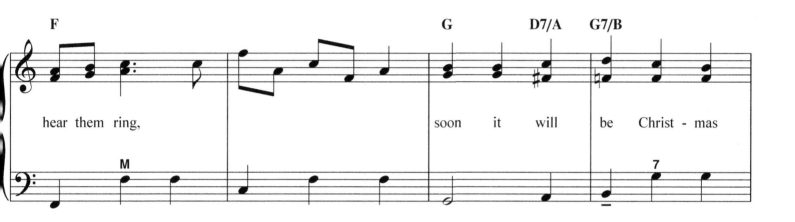

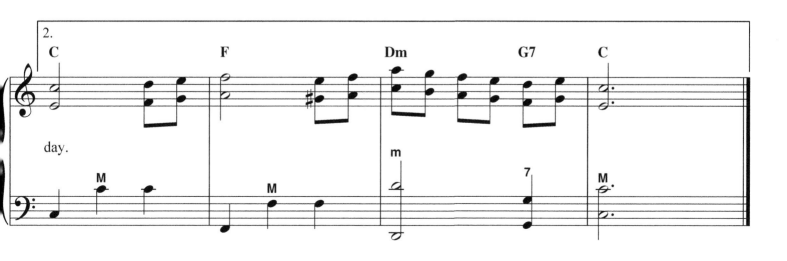

MY FAVORITE THINGS
from THE SOUND OF MUSIC

Lyrics by OSCAR HAMMERSTEIN II
Music by RICHARD RODGERS

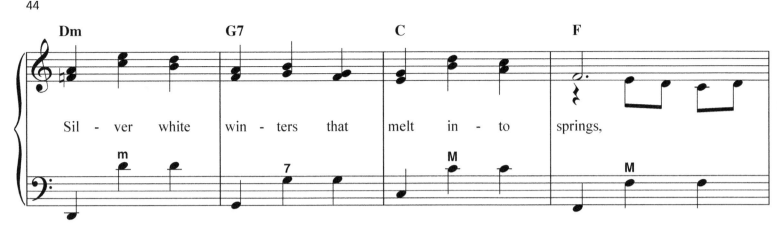

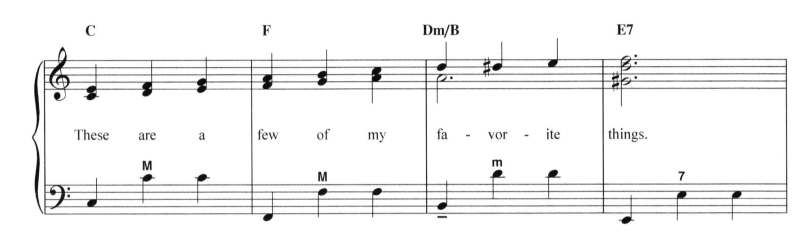

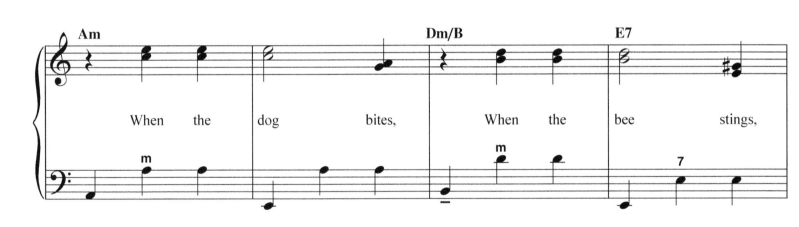

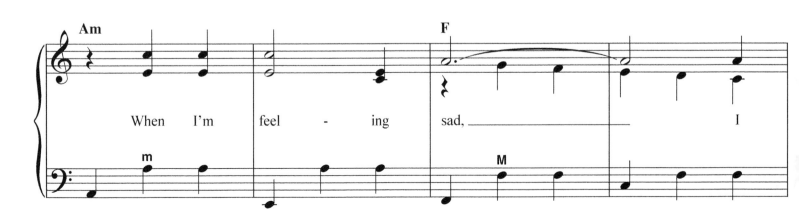

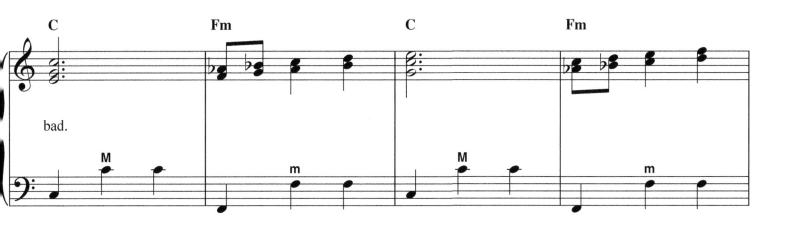

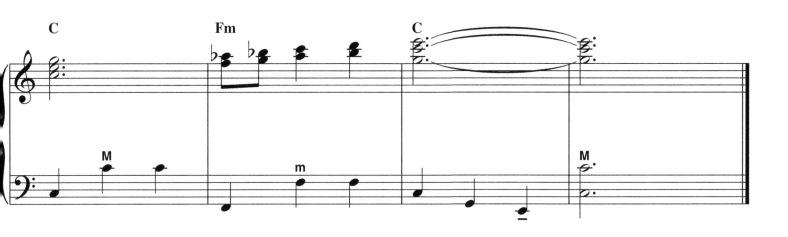

SLEIGH RIDE

Music by LEROY ANDERSON
Words by MITCHELL PARISH

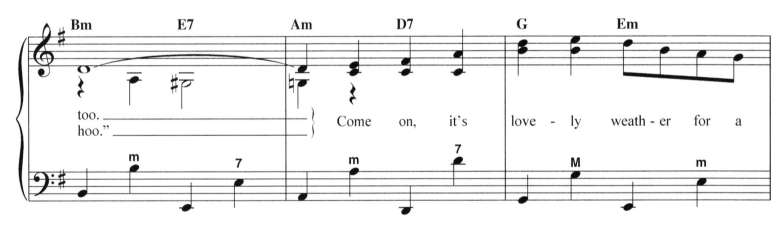

hand.   We're glid-ing a - long with a song of a win-ter-y fair-y -

land. Our cheeks are | nice and ros - y and | com - fy co - zy are
                 road be - fore us and | sing a cho - rus or

we. | We're snug - gled | up to - geth - er like two
two. | Come on, it's | love - ly weath - er for a

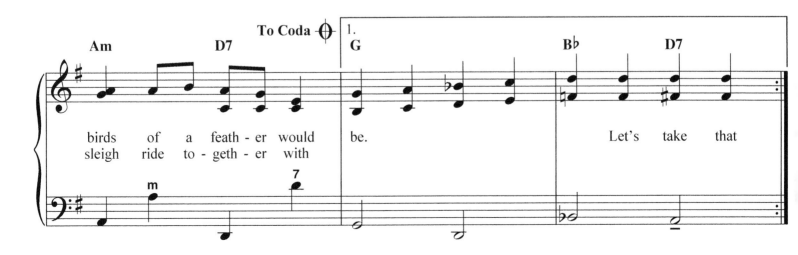

birds of a feath - er would | be. | Let's take that
sleigh ride to - geth - er with

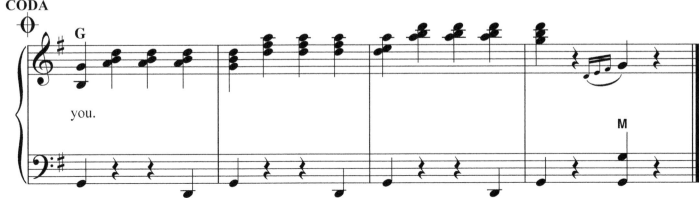

SNOWFALL

Lyrics by RUTH THORNHILL
Music by CLAUDE THORNHILL

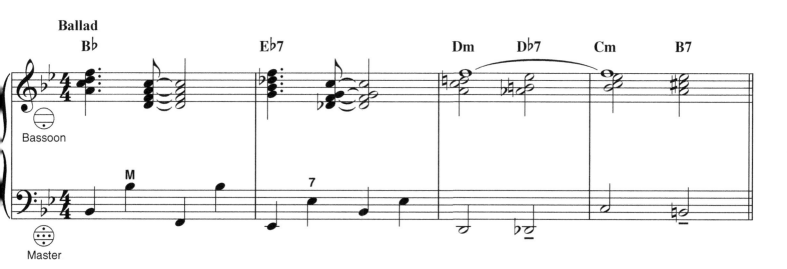

Snow - fall, _____ soft - ly, _____

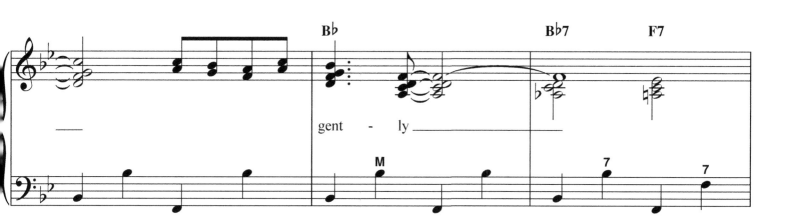

_____ gent - ly _____

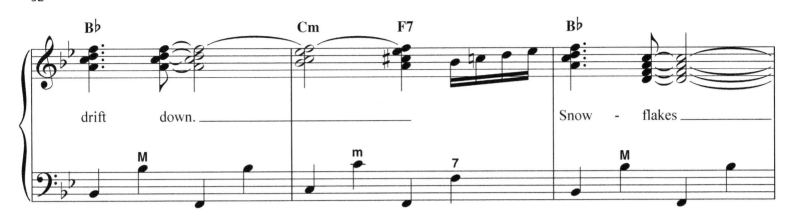

drift down._____ Snow - flakes _____

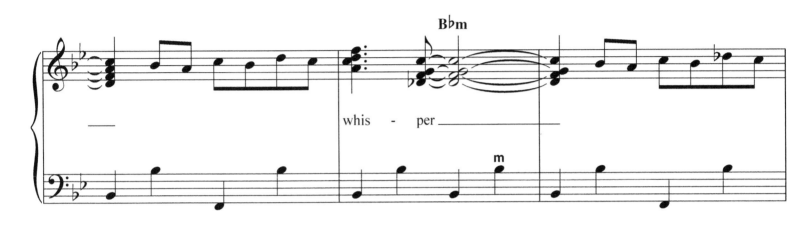

___ whis - per _____

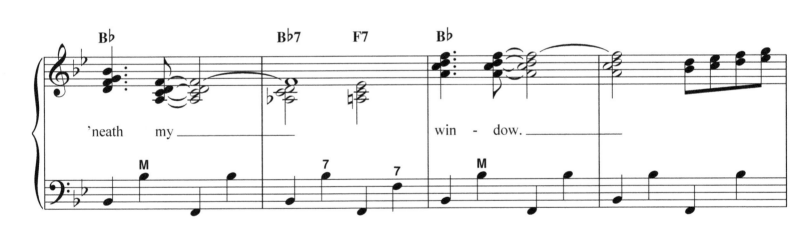

'neath my _____ win - dow. _____

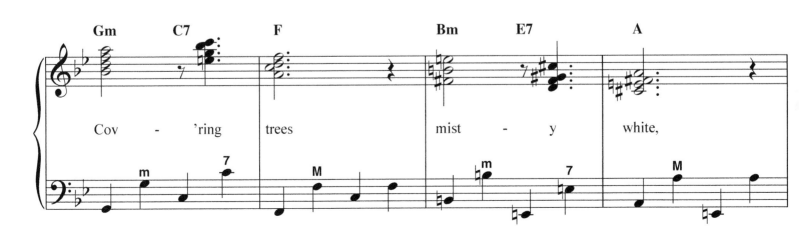

Cov - 'ring trees mist - y white,

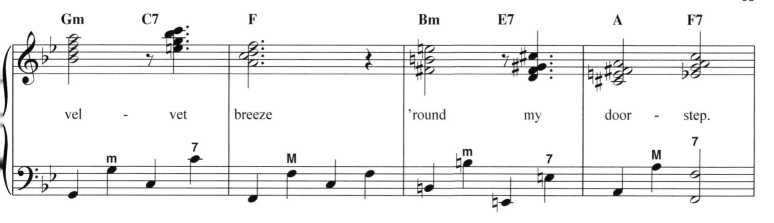

vel - vet   breeze   'round   my   door - step.

Gent - ly, _____   soft - ly, _____

si - lent _____   snow - fall! _____

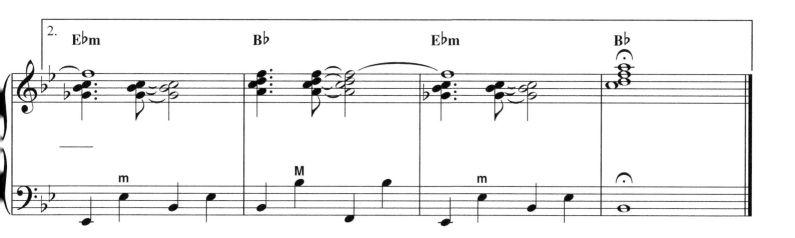

SOMEWHERE IN MY MEMORY

from the Twentieth Century Fox Motion Picture HOME ALONE

Words by LESLIE BRICUSSE
Music by JOHN WILLIAMS

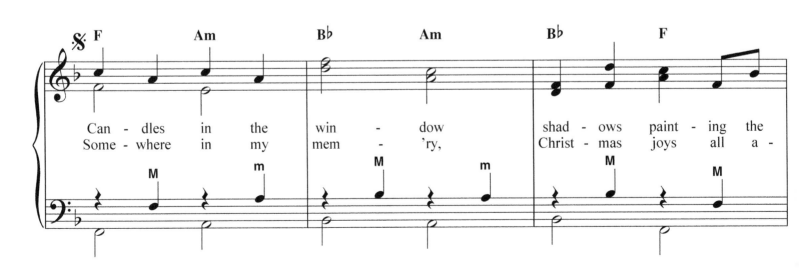

Can - dles in the win - dow
Some - where in my mem - 'ry,

shad - ows paint - ing the
Christ - mas joys all a -

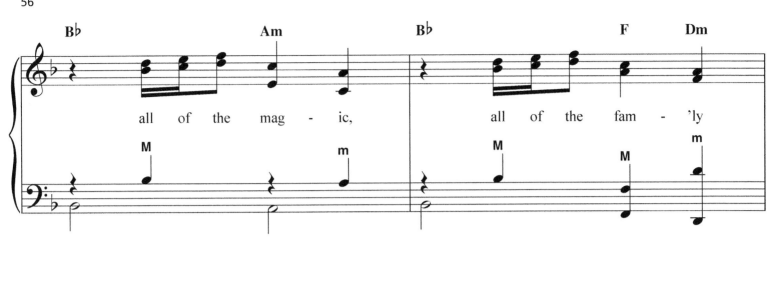

all of the mag - ic,   all of the fam - 'ly

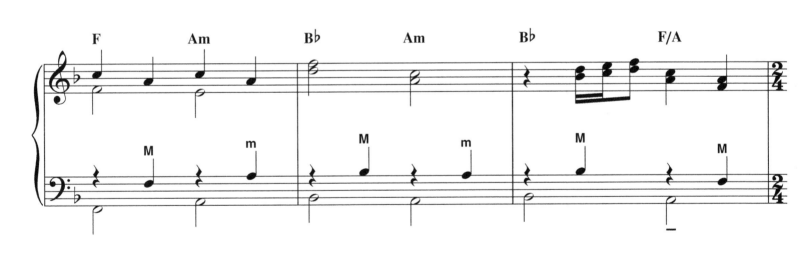

home here   with   me.

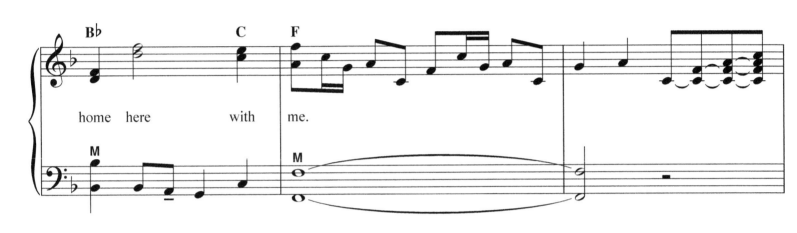

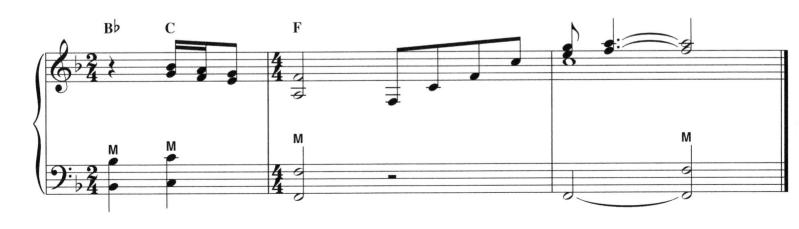

THIS CHRISTMAS

Words and Music by DONNY HATHAWAY
and NADINE McKINNOR

58

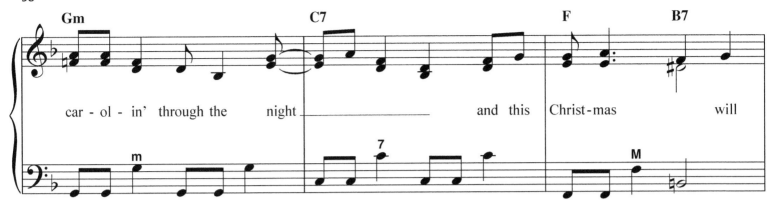

car - ol - in' through the night _____ and this Christ-mas will

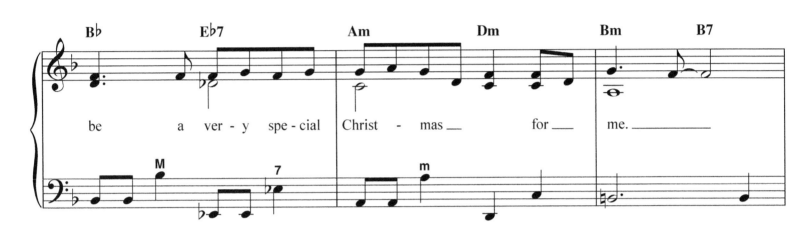

be a ver - y spe - cial Christ - mas __ for __ me. __

Mer - ry Christ-mas. __

WHITE CHRISTMAS
from the Motion Picture Irving Berlin's HOLIDAY INN

Words and Music by
IRVING BERLIN

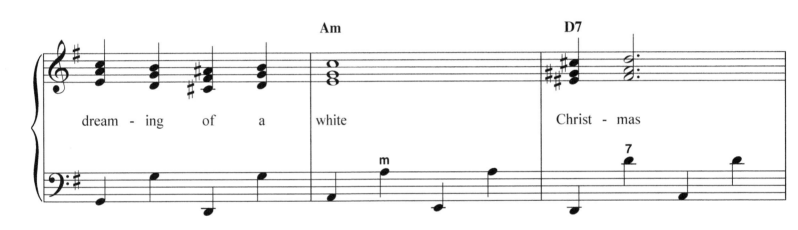

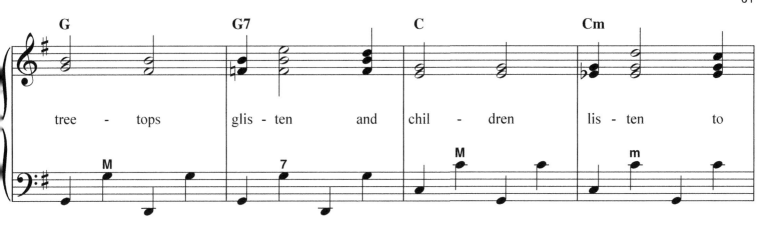

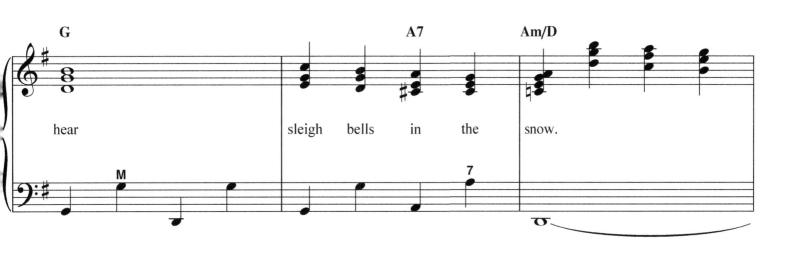

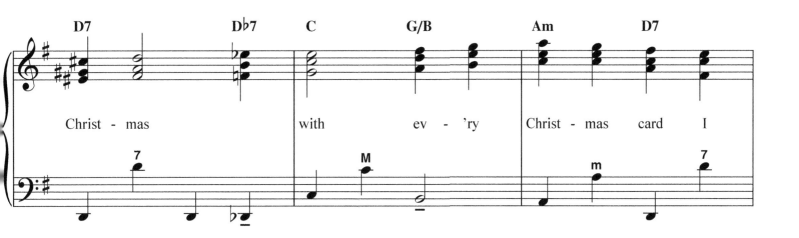

WINTER WONDERLAND

Words by DICK SMITH
Music by FELIX BERNARD

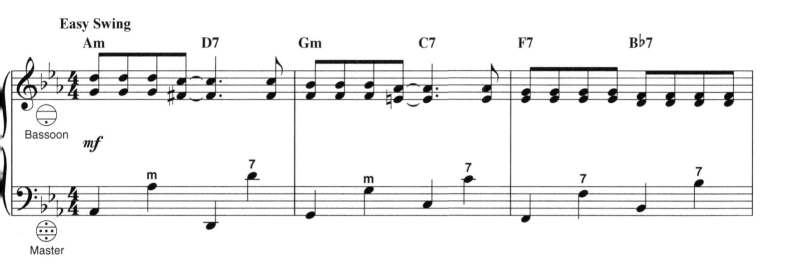

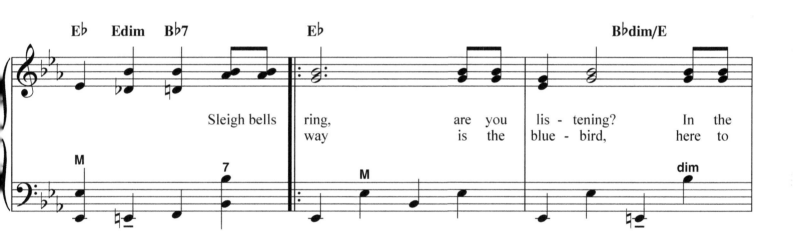

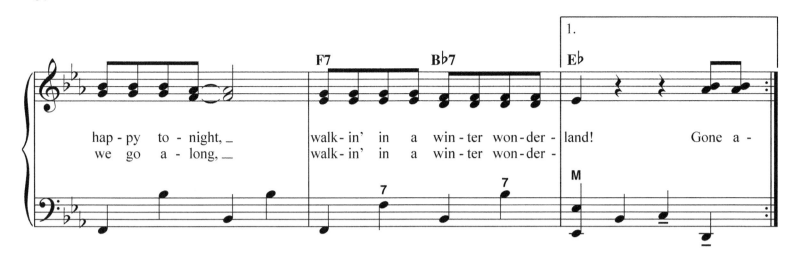

hap - py to - night, _ walk - in' in a win - ter won - der - land! Gone a -
we go a - long, _ walk - in' in a win - ter won - der -

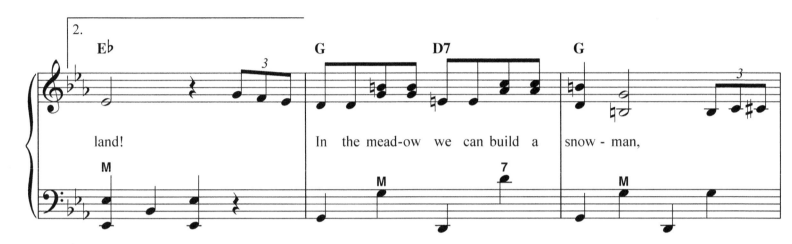

land! In the mead-ow we can build a snow - man,

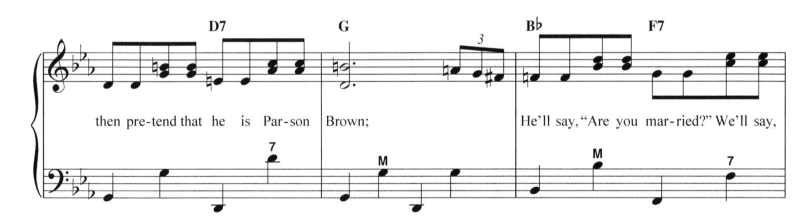

then pre-tend that he is Par-son Brown; He'll say, "Are you mar-ried?" We'll say,

"No, man! But you can do the job when you're in town!" La - ter

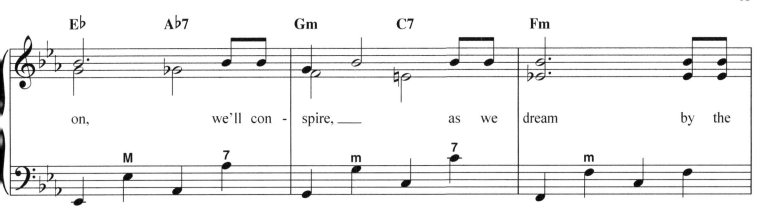

on,   we'll con - spire, _____ as we dream by the

fire, _____ to face un - a - fraid, _ the plans that we made, _

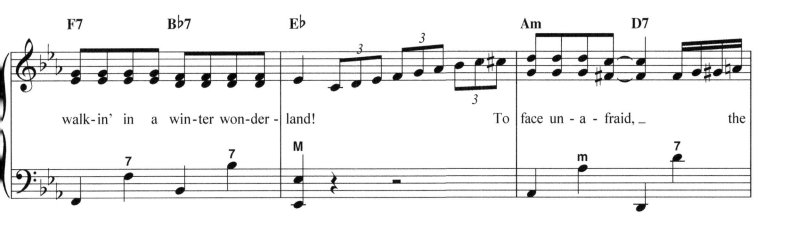

walk-in' in a win-ter won-der - land! To face un - a - fraid, _ the

plans that we made, _ walk-in' in a win-ter won-der - land!

WONDERFUL CHRISTMASTIME

Words and Music by
PAUL McCARTNEY

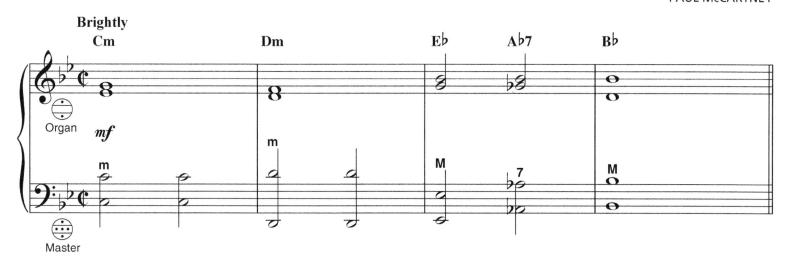

The mood is right, ___ the spir - it's up, ___
The par - ty's on, ___ the feel - ing's here ___
The word is out ___ a - bout the town ___

we're here to - night ___
that on - ly comes ___
to lift a glass, ___

68

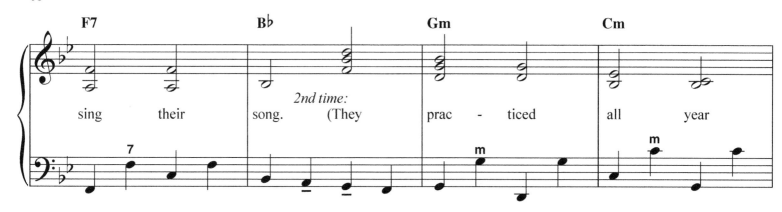

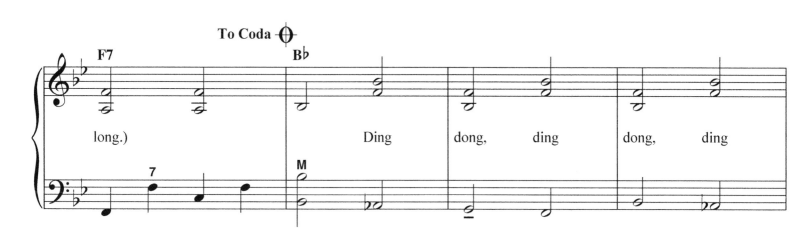

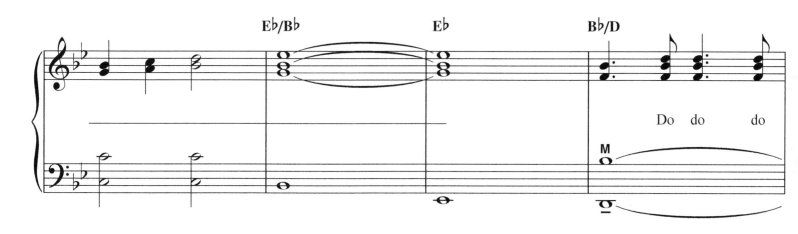

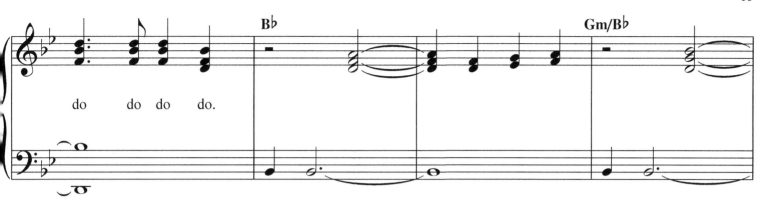

do   do do do.

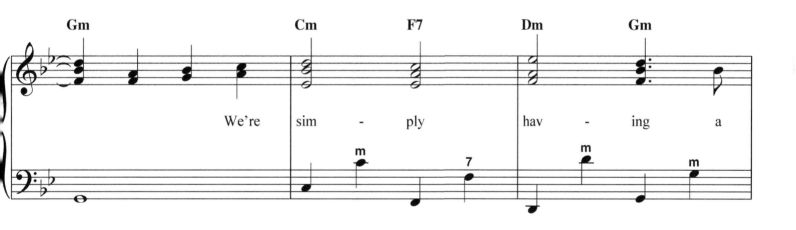

We're sim - ply   hav - ing   a

won - der - ful Christ - mas - time.   Sim - ply

70

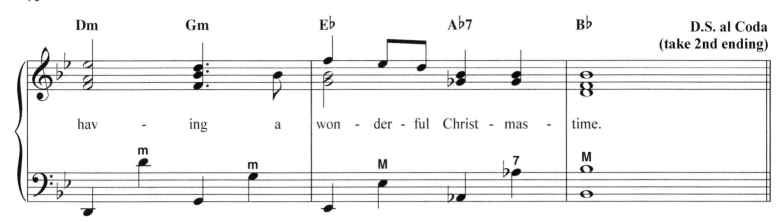

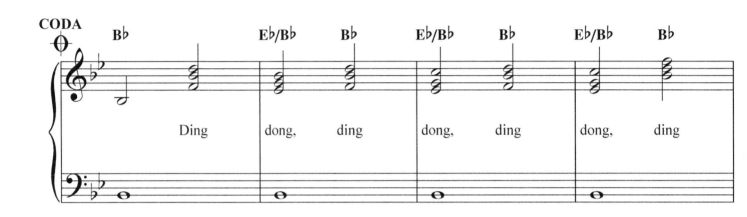

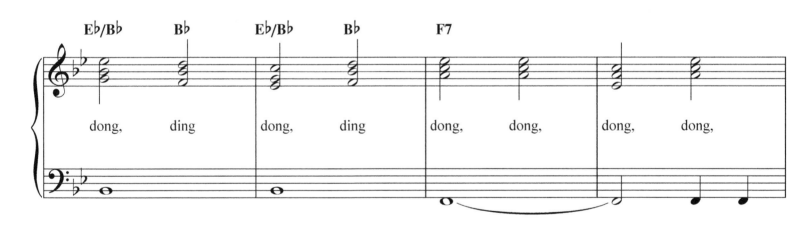

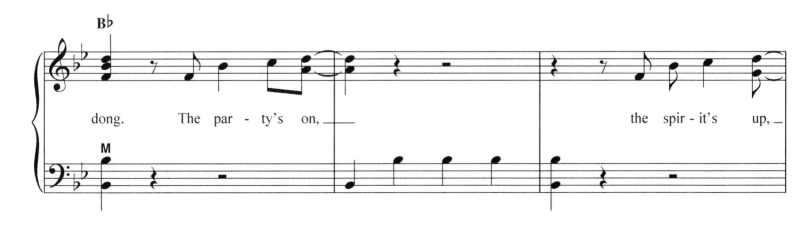

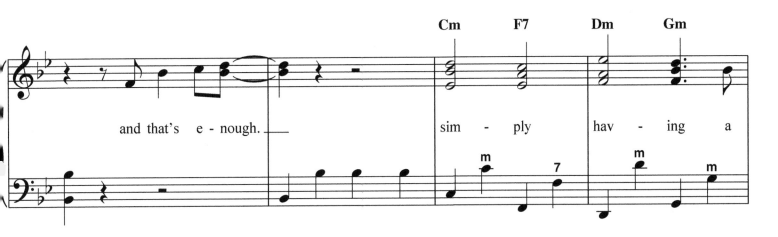

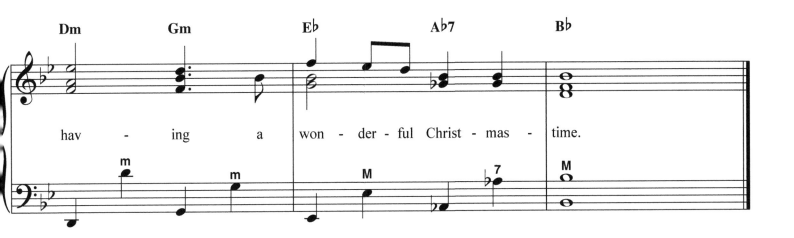

A COLLECTION OF ALL-TIME FAVORITES
FOR ACCORDION

ACCORDION FAVORITES
arr. Gary Meisner

16 all-time favorites, arranged for accordion, including: Can't Smile Without You • Could I Have This Dance • Endless Love • Memory • Sunrise, Sunset • I.O.U. • and more.
00359012...$12.99

ALL-TIME FAVORITES FOR ACCORDION
arr. Gary Meisner

20 must-know standards arranged for accordions. Includes: Ain't Misbehavin' • Autumn Leaves • Crazy • Hello, Dolly! • Hey, Good Lookin' • Moon River • Speak Softly, Love • Unchained Melody • The Way We Were • Zip-A-Dee-Doo-Dah • and more.
00311088...$12.99

THE BEATLES FOR ACCORDION

17 hits from the Lads from Liverpool have been arranged for accordion. Includes: All You Need Is Love • Eleanor Rigby • The Fool on the Hill • Here Comes the Sun • Hey Jude • In My Life • Let It Be • Ob-La-Di, Ob-La-Da • Penny Lane • When I'm Sixty-Four • Yesterday • and more.
00268724 ....$14.99

BROADWAY FAVORITES
arr. Ken Kotwitz

A collection of 17 wonderful show songs, including: Don't Cry for Me Argentina • Getting to Know You • If I Were a Rich Man • Oklahoma • People Will Say We're in Love • We Kiss in a Shadow.
00490157...$10.99

DISNEY SONGS FOR ACCORDION – 3RD EDITION

13 Disney favorites especially arranged for accordion, including: Be Our Guest • Beauty and the Beast • Can You Feel the Love Tonight • Chim Chim Cher-ee • It's a Small World • Let It Go • Under the Sea • A Whole New World • You'll Be in My Heart • Zip-A-Dee-Doo-Dah • and more!
00152508 ....$12.99

FIRST 50 SONGS YOU SHOULD PLAY ON THE ACCORDION
arr. Gary Meisner

If you're new to the accordion, you are probably eager to learn some songs. This book provides 50 simplified arrangements of must-know popular standards, folk songs and show tunes, including: All of Me • Beer Barrel Polka • Carnival of Venice • Edelweiss • Hava Nagila (Let's Be Happy) • Hernando's Hideaway • Jambalaya (On the Bayou) • Lady of Spain • Moon River • 'O Sole Mio • Sentimental Journey • Somewhere, My Love • That's Amore (That's Love) • Under Paris Skies • and more. Includes lyrics when applicable.
00250269 ....$16.99

FRENCH SONGS FOR ACCORDION
arr. Gary Meisner

A très magnifique collection of 17 French standards arranged for the accordion. Includes: Autumn Leaves • Beyond the Sea • C'est Magnifique • I Love Paris • La Marseillaise • Let It Be Me (Je T'appartiens) • Under Paris Skies • Watch What Happens • and more.
00311498...$10.99

HYMNS FOR ACCORDION
arr. Gary Meisner

24 treasured sacred favorites arranged for accordion, including: Amazing Grace • Beautiful Savior • Come, Thou Fount of Every Blessing • Crown Him with Many Crowns • Holy, Holy, Holy • It Is Well with My Soul • Just a Closer Walk with Thee • A Mighty Fortress Is Our God • Nearer, My God, to Thee • The Old Rugged Cross • Rock of Ages • What a Friend We Have in Jesus • and more.
00277160 ....$9.99

ITALIAN SONGS FOR ACCORDION
arr. Gary Meisner

17 favorite Italian standards arranged for accordion, including: Carnival of Venice • Ciribiribin • Come Back to Sorrento • Funiculi, Funicula • La donna è mobile • La Spagnola • 'O Sole Mio • Santa Lucia • Tarantella • and more.
00311089...$9.95

LATIN FAVORITES FOR ACCORDION
arr. Gary Meisner

20 Latin favorites, including: Bésame Mucho (Kiss Me Much) • The Girl from Ipanema • How Insensitive (Insensatez) • Perfidia • Spanish Eyes • So Nice (Summer Samba) • and more.
00310932...$14.99

THE FRANK MAROCCO ACCORDION SONGBOOK

This songbook includes arrangements and recordings of 15 standards and original songs from legendary jazz accordionist Frank Marocco, including: All the Things You Are • Autumn Leaves • Beyond the Sea • Moon River • Moonlight in Vermont • Stormy Weather (Keeps Rainin' All the Time) • and more!
00233441 Book/Online Audio...............$19.99

POP STANDARDS FOR ACCORDION
Arrangements of 20 Classic Songs

20 classic pop standards arranged for accordion are included in this collection: Annie's Song • Chances Are • For Once in My Life • Help Me Make It Through the Night • My Cherie Amour • Ramblin' Rose • (Sittin' On) The Dock of the Bay • That's Amore (That's Love) • Unchained Melody • and more.
00254822 ....$14.99

POLKA FAVORITES
arr. Kenny Kotwitz

An exciting new collection of 16 songs, including: Beer Barrel Polka • Liechtensteiner Polka • My Melody of Love • Paloma Blanca • Pennsylvania Polka • Too Fat Polka • and more.
00311573...$12.99

STAR WARS FOR ACCORDION

A dozen songs from the Star Wars franchise: The Imperial March (Darth Vader's Theme) • Luke and Leia • March of the Resistance • Princess Leia's Theme • Rey's Theme • Star Wars (Main Theme) • and more.
00157380 ....$14.99

TANGOS FOR ACCORDION
arr. Gary Meisner

Every accordionist needs to know some tangos! Here are 15 favorites: Amapola (Pretty Little Poppy) • Aquellos Ojos Verdes (Green Eyes) • Hernando's Hideaway • Jalousie (Jealousy) • Kiss of Fire • La Cumparsita (The Masked One) • Quizás, Quizás, Quizás (Perhaps, Perhaps, Perhaps) • The Rain in Spain • Tango of Roses • Whatever Lola Wants (Lola Gets) • and more!
00122252 ....$9.99

3-CHORD SONGS FOR ACCORDION
arr. Gary Meisner

Here are nearly 30 songs that are easy to play but still sound great! Includes: Amazing Grace • Can Can • Danny Boy • For He's a Jolly Good Fellow • He's Got the Whole World in His Hands • Just a Closer Walk with Thee • La Paloma Blanca (The White Dove) • My Country, 'Tis of Thee • Ode to Joy • Oh! Susanna • Yankee Doodle • The Yellow Rose of Texas • and more.
00312104 ....$12.99

LAWRENCE WELK'S POLKA FOLIO

More than 50 famous polkas, schottisches and waltzes arranged for piano and accordion, including: Blue Eyes • Budweiser Polka • Clarinet Polka • Cuckoo Polka • The Dove Polka • Draw One Polka • Gypsy Polka • Helena Polka • International Waltzes • Let's Have Another One • Schnitzelbank • Shuffle Schottische • Squeeze Box Polka • Waldteuful Waltzes • and more.
00123218...$12.99

HAL•LEONARD®
Visit Hal Leonard Online at
www.halleonard.com